# VENICE
# PAST AND PRESENT

# VENICE
## PAST AND PRESENT
### TEXT BY
### SELWYN BRINTON, M.A.

*Author of "The Renaissance in Italian Art"*

### EDITED BY GEOFFREY HOLME
### LONDON: THE STUDIO LTD., 44 LEICESTER SQUARE, W.C.2
### 1925

Printed and Engraved by Herbert
Reiach, Ltd., Eyot Works, St.
Peter's Square, Hammersmith,
London, W.6

# CONTENTS

## INTRODUCTION

## LIST OF ILLUSTRATIONS

(* Denotes Illustrations in Colour)

## CHURCHES AND PUBLIC BUILDINGS

## QUAYS, BRIDGES AND GARDENS

## EDITORIAL NOTE.

The Editor desires to express his thanks to the authorities of the British and Foreign Museums who have kindly given facilities for the reproduction of the illustrations included in this volume; to H. B. Burney, Esq., Signor M. Crespi, Campbell Dodgson, Esq., C.B.E., Michael Holroyd, Esq., Axel Jacobsen, Esq., Herman Lamm, Esq., H. Yates Thompson, Esq., Sir Robert C. Witt, Mme. Anders Zorn; and to Messrs. Thomas Agnew & Sons, Messrs. G. & P. Alinari, Max Rothschild, Esq., of The Sackville Gallery, D. Croal Thomson, Esq., and Messrs. Arthur Tooth & Sons, Ltd.

# CHAPTER I

## THE PALACE AND THE BASILICA

UT of the waves came Venice—a thing seaborn, like the Cyprian goddess of old legend. This thought came to my mind when first I touched on my subject here; and yesterday I found it expressed, in words I could not better, by the writer of a delightful study on her seacharm.[1] "Venice, among Italian towns, stands alone. She only is built, not by the sea, but in the sea; born, not on the beach of ocean, but like Aphrodite, from beneath her heart"; and he goes on to show how the "mighty being" of the sea penetrates and pervades all the life of the old city, how her streets are streams of the sea and planned by its will, how the great path which, curling like a serpent, divides the city is but a sea-river; and how the waters that make her unique are tidal waters, beautiful in themselves, full of vital movement, streaming in at the openings of her "lidi," at the ports of Malamocco, Chioggia, Lido, Tre Porti, filling the lagoon with incessant movement, with clashing sweeping currents. In the midst of all this lies Venice herself, in the heart of this water-world, of this blue or shimmering expanse, in summer days asleep "like a miracle of opal or pearl upon the bosom of an undulating lake"; her own sea, guarded by long banks of sand through which the tide arrives, is tempered into quietness from the turbulence without—her lagoon, the mirror of the clouds and sky, scattered with islands, "outstretched like sea-creatures" upon its silvery waters.

Full of their own quiet charm are these islands of the lagoon, their very names bringing to us a fragrance of the past—S. Lazzaro, Sta. Elena, S. Giacomo della Palude, S. Giorgio in Alga, S. Francesco del Deserto. Once they had each their monastic church, whose bells sounded at vespers across the lagoon: two only remain, in S. Lazzaro and St. Francis of the Desert, whose cypresses still guard the cloister and the old convent church. But now I would have my reader, rowing out into the lagoon, turn his gondola—leaving the Lido and its bathers on the right, then Murano with her Cathedral, Burano, and Chioggia in the vaporous distance—to where Torcello awaits us, with her ancient Cathedral and Church of Sta. Fosca. For here we are in touch with the very beginnings of Venetian story. Here those fugitives from Aquileia and Altinum on the mainland had sought a shelter from the wave of barbarism which in the fifth century was blotting out the old civilisation, and making their homes a heap of ashes; and in the mosaics

[1] "The Sea-charm of Venice," by Stopford A. Brooke.

1

here of the Cathedral, in the scene of Judgment and that solemn and most beautiful Virgin, we may see pictured in Byzantine forms of art their cry to Heaven, united in their memories, in their common misfortune, in their Christian faith. " Built "—says Ruskin of this Duomo of Torcello—" by men in flight and distress, who sought in the hurried erection of their island church a shelter for their earnest and sorrowful worship . . . men persecuted but not forsaken, cast down but not destroyed "; and he adds that he is "not aware of any other early church in Italy which has this expression in so marked a degree."[1] But among this group of Christian exiles slowly the germs of a new civic life, always Roman in its tradition, never once brought under the invader's power, was beginning to bloom again into new forms of life.

Such were the conditions under which Venice developed, a slow growth, of many centuries, as of something wonderful, perfect in itself—from that group of stricken fugitives into that glorious Empire City, the Queen of the Adriatic. At first a colony of Padua, as the daughter grows into young new life, under the mother's protection, gradually she frees herself. In 466 the little community meets at Grado to elect its own tribunes : in 523 Cassiodorus, Chancellor of the Gothic King Theodoric, describes their dwellings, spread like sea-birds' nests, half on sea, half on land. " The poor man there "—he tells us—" is equal of the rich ; their houses are alike, there are no differences among them, no jealousies." Mazzorbo, Burano, Murano, Malamocco had now been added : then, at the farthest line of the deep curving channel, Rivo Alto, on whose islands the Venetians were to set their capital. For here was to be built, to blossom into its later glory, their Ducal Palace ; and already in 697, the first Doge had been elected chief of the Venetian State. The earliest Palace was that erected, soon after 900, by Doge Participazio, and repaired and enlarged, late in the twelfth century by Doge Ziani : while Sansovino tells us that " in 1301, under Doge Gradenigo, was commenced the Hall of the Great Council, and finished in 1309."

Only a few years before this the same great Council had become the real masters of Venice by the decree proposed in 1296, and established in 1299, known as the " Serrata del Consiglio." For, on the funeral of Dandolo, ten years earlier, the people, recalling their rights of election, had clamoured for Giacomo Tiepolo as their Doge. But in his stead Gradenigo had been elected, and their share in the Government taken away, and given to a Council limited to families inscribed in the Book of Gold. The popular discontent at these measures found expression in a rising under Bajamonte Tiepolo, which was crushed by the Doge and Council ; and in 1310 the Tribunal known as the Council of Ten was

[1] " Stones of Venice," by John Ruskin. Vol. II, Ch. 2.

2

created, its first decree being to demolish the houses of the Tiepolo and Querini. Intended as a temporary measure, this powerful Council became permanent, and gave its peculiar character to the Venetian oligarchy. Even the Doge himself became its servant. When, as was inevitable, the popular resentment again found expression, this time in 1355, with the Doge himself, Marin Faliero, as leader of the plot, on the very eve of its fulfilment he was suddenly arrested and haled before this terrible tribunal of justice. Confronted with his confederates he confessed. On the balcony of the Palace stood forth one of the Ten, a bloody sword in his hand, who cried aloud to the people—" Justice has been done on the traitor! " Then the gates of the inner court were opened, and the crowd, pressing forward, saw on the ground before them the severed head of their Doge, Marin Faliero. In the acts of the Ten, where this record should appear, are only the words—" Let it not be written." In the long line of the portraits of Doges of Venice, within that grand Sala del Maggiore Consiglio of the Ducal Palace, one is covered with a black veil, that of Marin Faliero—" decapitatus pro criminibus."

With this lesson before him the Venetian citizen found it wiser henceforth to leave government in the hands of the oligarchy, whose strong rule held Venice in its grasp, and was to steer the ship of State in future, through the fiercely contested duel of Venice with Genoa, for trade sea-power, even for existence itself, up to the days of her power on the mainland, and the establishment of her supreme position as mistress of the trade of the East and of the southern seas. But his acquiescence came from higher motives than merely prudence or indifference. Venice, it has been remarked—not alone in her beginnings, but in constitution, in her laws, tradition, the temper of her citizens, in manners, in her greatness, her splendour, even in her unbridled luxury and decay was Roman to the end[1]; and Henri Taine has said[2] that the citizen who felt himself as a part of this Venice—a hamlet of fishing folk planted on the mud, without land, water, stone or wood, yet who conquered the cities of her gulf, then Constantinople, the Peloponnesus, Cyprus—of this Venice who could crush seven revolts at Zara and sixteen in Crete, could defeat Dalmatians, Byzantines, the Sultans of Cairo and the Kings of Hungary, could send into the Bosphorus fleets of five hundred sails, arm squadrons of two hundred galleys, by her fleets of galleons bring together Trebizond, Alexandria, Tunis, Tangier, Lisbon and London; and, last of all, create industries, an architecture, painting and manners of her own, and transform herself into a magnificent jewel of art—this Venetian citizen felt indeed a Roman

[1] Cf. Stopford A Brooke. Op. Cit.
[2] V. H. Taine. " Voyage en Italie." Vol. II. Venise.

3

pride in his city, in her achievements and her destiny, felt of her as something to be lived for and died for, to be worshipped with a personal and passionate devotion.

Most of all did this feeling centre around the Palace of her Doge— "the home of the Most Serene Republic," the visible symbol of her greatness, the shrine wherein Venezia abode enthroned. The earlier Palace was commenced, as we have seen (the date, however, in the Savin Chronicle is 810)—about the same time as the Basilica of S. Marco by Doge Participazio, when Rialto had been made the seat of government; and, as Ruskin has pointed out very clearly, was built successively in three styles. "There was a Byzantine Ducal Palace, a Gothic Ducal Palace and a Renaissance Ducal Palace. The second superseded the first totally. . . . But the third superseded the second in part only, and the existing building is formed by the union of the two." The Gothic Palace was begun—as I have mentioned—with the Hall of the Great Council in 1301, and the work was continued for more than a century, while, piece by piece, the older Byzantine Palace of Ziani was being swallowed up into the new and glorious structure. A prison (" Gheba " or " Gabbia "—the fact is suggestive) was added after the Council of Ten appeared on the scene. Then the beautiful gate now replaced by the Porta della Carta was added by Doge Dandolo, where—says the Savin Chronicle—" is his statue, on his knees with the standard in his hand, before the Lion of St. Mark." Finally the Hall of the Great Council, still in existence, on whose walls Guariento painted (in 1365) his " Paradiso " (to be replaced later by Tintoretto's vision of Paradise), though the roof, then showing the heavens covered with stars, was not completed until 1400.

But in 1419 Doge Mocenigo rose in the Council, braving the fine threatening any who proposed further change, to propose that the remaining structure be rebuilt " in a way more fitting the greatness to which, by God's grace, their dominions had reached "; and within the next twenty years the Gothic Palace must have been completed in the form we now see—a vast oblong, with its sides facing the Piazzetta and Riva dei Schiavoni available for the most sumptuous external decoration. Here, then, the Venetian Architect-Sculptors had poured forth all their most delightful imagery. Worthy of separate study are these capitals of their columns, adorned with delicate foliage, heads of children, of women, of warriors, the Virtues and Vices, the wise men of old, the months of the year—a whole imagery of life itself reflected in the stone. Famous are the figures and groups at the angles —the Archangels, the figures of Justice, of Adam and Eve, the groups of the " Drunkenness of Noah " or the " Judgment of Solomon "— each most often suggesting some spiritual truth, some moral or civic

4

lesson.   There must have been a series of architects engaged in this glorious creation, among whom a chief part has been given to Filippo Calendario, who was said to have been involved in the conspiracy of the Doge Marin Faliero, and to have been hung, with his sons and father-in-law, from that balcony of the Palace which he may himself have designed.   This legend has been questioned by later critics, and Molmenti mentions Pietro Baseggio and Maestro Enrico, with the title of Proto del Comune, as leading figures in the construction : while the Venetian family of Buono were the sculptor-architects of the beautiful Porta Dorata or Porta della Carta.

I shall refer in the next chapter to those paintings within the Palace, which form an integral part of the splendour of Venice ; and I turn now to the Basilica of S. Marco, whose creation we find to have been contemporaneous with that of the Palace itself.   In a wonderful passage —but one which does not perhaps altogether lose by being shortened— Ruskin has pictured the impression of that first view of St. Mark's façade from the angle at the far end of the Square, the Bocca di Piazza. " Between those pillars there opens a great light, and, in the midst of it the vast tower of St. Mark seems to lift itself bodily forth . . . and, on each side, the countless arches prolong themselves into ranged symmetry. Beyond those ordered arches there rises a vision out of the earth. . . a multitude of pillars and white domes, clustered into a long low pyramid of coloured light ; a treasure heap, it seems, partly of gold and partly of opal and mother-of-pearl, hollowed beneath into five great vaulted porches, ceiled with fair mosaic, and beset with sculpture of alabaster, clear as amber and delicate as ivory—sculpture fantastic and involved, of palm leaves and lilies, and grapes and pomegranates, and birds cling- ing and fluttering. . . all twined together, and in the midst the solemn forms of angels, sceptred, and robed to the feet, leaning to each other across the gates, their figures indistinct among the gleaming of the golden ground."

But it is when we have passed beneath this portico and entered within the church itself that this impression of Eastern richness, of colour and mystery, becomes intensified.   For we find ourselves in a shrine where the light only enters vaguely—diffused, reflected from the walls of rose-toned marbles, and that dim gold of the mosaics above and around.   The main fabric dates from the rule of Doge Contarini, who (1063) commenced the reconstruction, changing its design from the old Basilican type into that of a Greek cross, and using most probably Byzantine artists, helped by Lombard or Venetian craftsmen, the whole blending together to form a new and unique style, which has been called Veneto-Byzantine.   The core of the fabric was of brick, to which how- ever had been superadded or veneered rich marbles from the Greek

5

cities of the Empire, alabaster from the Orient, sculpture and the colour and gold of the mosaic work. Sometimes the older columns—the plunder of Venetian galleys, like those horses of St. Mark without, brought from the Hippodrome of Byzantium—were sliced and reversed, but more often set in their new home intact ; and Ruskin, whose study of this earlier period is priceless, entirely approves the system. " The Venetians were exiles from beautiful and ancient cities, and had been accustomed to build with their ruins, not less in affection than in admiration ; they had thus not only grown familiar with the practice of inserting older fragments in modern buildings, but they owed to that practice a great part of the splendour of their city. . . . The practice which began in the affections of a fugitive nation was prolonged in the pride of a conquering one ; and beside the memorials of departed happiness were elevated the trophies of returning victory."

The result seen in the entrance, and still more in the church itself, is indescribable : it is emotional, and words can here only suggest. Darkness and mystery, vague recesses of shadow, gleams of sudden light, reflected from cool transparent alabaster, from polished marbles or from lustrous gold. Two colours emerge here as dominant, that of the rose-veined marbles of the walls or columns, and that of the gold of the mosaics, whose edges catch and hold imprisoned the gleams of light. " Red upon gold "—exclaims Taine—" and all in shadow." " Rouge sur or, et dans l'ombre : on ne s'imagine pas un pareil ton." And this subdued Eastern splendour of the church finds its culmination in her Pala d'Oro, which is exposed at Easter, enamelled work of silver and gold set with gems, the work of craftsmen of Byzantium ; and brought thence, like the bronze horses, by the Venetian galleys, though some of the more precious jewels were taken by the French upon the fall of the Republic.

The Campanile, which soars up from the Piazza without, dates back to the defeat of the Hungarian invaders, under Doge Pietro Tribuno (900), and may have been useful to the city, not only for its bells, but also for a watch-tower across the lagoons. I was present at its consecration when it had been rebuilt, and shall never forget the scene when the bells, so long silent, rang out again, and the startled pigeons, as if to greet them, flew up into the light ; the emotion of the Venetian people upon that day, and in that wonderful moment, was real and impressive.

From the first the art of Venice shows the love of colour, of Eastern warmth and glow which we have traced within her shrine of St. Mark. Late in its appearance it had remained almost uninfluenced by the presence at Padua of Giotto and his new message in art ; though the great painting by Guariento in the Hall of the Great Council—which I

6

was able to see years ago when Tintoretto's " Paradise " was removed— has been found to show traces of Giottesque influence.   But this art of Venice begins to develop its individual character under the Vivarini and the painters of Murano, who are the real beginners of the school, even when the early work of Semitecolo, Lorenzo Veneziano and Jacobello del Fiore (Venice Academy) must not be overlooked.   With the Vivarini, Antonio and Bartolommeo, the drawing is formal and precise, gilding is freely introduced, richness of effect always sought after.   " It is mosaic "—I have written of the altarpiece at S. Zaccaria —" feeling its way to painting ; the magnificent material, the glowing gold laid on the clear blue, still dominating the dainty solemn painted figures."

But now came Gentile da Fabriano from Florence, with Pisanello at his side, to decorate the Ducal Palace : his influence is a strong one in this movement, both directly and yet more indirectly through his pupil Jacopo Bellini.   For Jacopo had served his apprenticeship to art under Gentile as his " famulus," had returned with him to Florence, had even named after his beloved master his eldest son Gentile : yet again the daughter of this Jacopo, Niccolosa, had married the Paduan Master, Andrea Mantegna, so that from this side, too, the art of the mainland (actually of Florence, if we consider that Mantegna had derived from the Paduan work of Donatello) poured now in a full enriching stream into this backward and secluded art of the city of the waters.   The result was a sudden and marvellous expansion—the creation, one might say, almost within one generation of a school of art individual, unsurpassed even in the Italy of that time.   From this timid, almost primitive art of the earlier Vivarini—which reaches perhaps its highest in Bartolommeo's magnificent triptych of the Frari, and becomes most expressive in his pupil or kinsman Alvise's lovely Virgin enthroned with Saints of the Venice Academy—we pass quickly through this Jacopo Bellini (whose sketch book, showing Mantegna's influence, is one of the treasures of our British Museum) to the Venetian pageant paintings of his son Gentile ; then to the yet completer art of Giovanni Bellini, the teacher of Titian and Giorgione, who takes us at one step into the richest creative period of Venetian painting, and whose story I reserve for my succeeding chapter.

7

# CHAPTER II

## THE SPLENDOUR OF VENICE

ENICE was then approaching the zenith of her power and splendour, and must in those days have been a most enchanting city. She had the whole trade of the East within her grasp, and touched with her merchant fleets on the one side Byzantium and Asia, on the other Flanders and England. In the early fifteenth century she seemed on the full tide of her expansion, her land and sea empire. Dalmatia, that former nest of pirates, was hers, and the banner of St. Mark floated over Zara. In 1404 she occupied Vicenza, in 1405 Verona, and later, in 1406, the city of Padua formally gave herself to Venice : she touched the Alps with Friuli and Cadore, was mistress of the Adriatic, and held Corfu, Corinth and later Cyprus.[1] Every year her great trading fleets, some five hundred vessels in each, sailed forth for Greece and Byzantium, Egypt and Africa, Flanders and England. The cargo of any one of these Syrian or Egyptian galleys was reckoned at 200,000 ducats ; they held accommodation for eight young nobles, to train in sea craft and commerce, and every man aboard must fight if needed. It was reckoned in those days that the Most Serene Republic could dispose of 3,300 ships, 36,000 seamen, and 16,000 shipwrights : later, when the Turkish peril became a menace in the East, she equipped a State navy of warships (*navi armate*) to act as convoys.

It is true that the policy of mainland expansion, to which she was now becoming committed, was a danger and a drain on her resources.[2] Her great Doge Tomaso Mocenigo, to whose generosity and public spirit was due the re-erection of the Ducal Palace, saw this danger clearly ; and on his death-bed in 1423, when after nine years of power he left his beloved city at the height of her glory, he solemnly warned the Senate against the election of Foscari, whose ambition he distrusted, as his successor. The warning was neglected ; and Venice, plunged by Francesco Foscari (1423-1457) into a long and exhausting war on the mainland, found, when the moment came to face the Turk and save Byzantium, that her resources were unequal to the task required of her.

But for the moment all seemed well as before. In the city the magnificent Hall of the Great Council was completed, the Porta della Carta added to the glories of the Ducal Palace ; in the East the city of Salonica (a fatal acquisition, which brought trouble with the Turk, and plague to the city) was added to her possessions ; in Italy she acquired

[1] See " The Story of Venice," by Thomas Okey. Ch. 7.
[2] " Venice." (Story of Nations), by Alethea Wiel. Ch. 10.

Ravenna, and held her own against the intrigues and power of the Visconti despot. Even later when De Comines entered Venice, by " the great street, which they call the Grand Canal . . . the fairest street that may be in the whole world, and fitted with the best houses . . . the ancient ones all painted, others faced with white marble, with many a great piece of porphyry or serpentine on their front," this stranger from the feudal north is filled with enthusiastic admiration.

" The most triumphant city," thus he writes to his prince, " that I have seen, and which doeth most honour to ambassadors and strangers, and where God's service is most solemnly done." For religion in Venice, who kept always her independence in front of Rome, was not only a matter of deep personal feeling (we trace this in her art and story), but a great function, in which the State claimed its part. Twelve times in the year the Doge, as head of the State, must make his solemn procession through the city on the great feasts of the Church ; the most famous being that of Ascension, when he went forth in the Bucentaur, steered by the high Admiral and followed by a thousand smaller craft, past Lido into the Adriatic to celebrate the wedding of Venice with the sea, with the sacramental words—" Sea, we espouse thee, in sign of true and everlasting dominion." Many of the lesser " andate " had political significance, recalling the past story of Venice : that of mid-June, the suppression (v. Ch. I) of the plot of Tiepolo ; that of July 17th, the recovery of Padua, after the League of Cambrai ; of October 15th, the taking of Famagosta ; and on St. Nicholas Day, that of Constantinople itself, captured by the Venetian Dandolo.

Pageantry thus formed an integral part of the Venetian's life, visualising for him the story and the splendour of his city ; and hence pageant painting was from the first a favourite subject. The great paintings of Venetian story within the Ducal Palace by Gentile da Fabriano, Alvise Vivarini and Gentile Bellini had all perished in successive fires ; but there remain to us three great canvases by the elder Bellini, Gentile, showing the " Procession of Corpus Domini," the " Miracles of the True Cross " (both these in the Venice Academy) and " The Preaching of St. Mark " (Brera Gallery). When Gentile died in 1507, he left the last-named painting to his brother Giovanni Bellini, together with their father's sketch-book, which I have already mentioned.

Gentile's position at Venice must have been a high one for him to have been employed (1474) by the State to restore his namesake's—da Fabriano's—paintings in the Ducal Palace, and to have been sent (in 1479) by the Senate to Constantinople, where he painted Sultan Mahomet's portrait ; but a discussion on a point of art criticism with that

9

monarch, who illustrated his view by having a slave then and there beheaded, led our artist to hurry forward his return journey. As a pageant painter Gentile, good as he is, is surpassed by his pupil Vittore Carpaccio, whose pictured stories (not true fresco, but painted on canvas) of St. Ursula (now in the Venice Academy) and of SS. George, Tryphonius and Jerome (S. Giorgio degli Schiavoni) possesses an imaginative quality, a suggestion of romance which neither Gentile, Giovanni Mansueti, nor indeed any of his Venetian contemporaries ever equalled. Full of interest is his scene (also in the Venice Academy) of the "History of the Cross," of the Canal thronged with gondolas while the Patriarch and his clergy carry the relics to an adjoining Palace; and yet more delightful is his meeting of St. Ursula (the background here quite Venetian in character) with the fair-haired Prince of Britain; or her interview with her father (this scene appears again in our National Gallery); or, most characteristic of all, the scene of her dream where she lies asleep in bed, every detail of the room painted with appreciative charm, while an angel enters into her dream world with the message of her coming martyrdom. But in his "Presentation of Christ" in the same Gallery he rises to the full height of his power to give us a grand canvas, which rivals even Giovanni Bellini, and where the exquisite child angels, who make soft music beneath Madonna and her group of girl attendants, possess this master's idyllic quality, and suggest themes which reappear throughout Venetian art.

With Carpaccio's contemporary, Giovanni Bellini, we find ourselves at once in the full stream of the complete Venetian art; for this painter, the greatest at Venice of his time, comes now to link the earlier Murano tradition with those supreme masters of the Venetian school, Titian, Giorgione, and their contemporaries and successors, Palma Vecchio, Lorenzo Lotto, Paris Bordone, Bonifazio, Veronese, Tintoretto. Enough of Mantegna's influence had come into his art to give it strength of design. We may trace this clearly in his "Christ's Agony in the Garden" of our own Gallery, comparing it with Mantegna's rendering there of the same subject, both paintings taken from a sketch by Jacopo Bellini; but the new message of the glory of Venetian colour, suggested already in the mosaics of St. Mark and Muranese paintings, is breaking through and finding its definite expression in his art. Giovanni, like his brother, Gentile Bellini, was occupied in the paintings of the Ducal Palace, and held there the office of superintendent; but this kind of subject never appealed to him strongly, and the opportunity which came to him of acquiring from Antonello da Messina the new practice of oil painting gave him just the medium he needed. His subject of predilection is the Virgin with her Babe, often with saintly persons, male or female, in attendance, and with the

10

loveliest child angels who make soft music beneath the steps of her throne. A treatment this, as I have noted already, which is frequent in Venetian art; but it remains unsurpassed in Giovanni's Madonna enthroned, with child angels below, of the Frari Church, and in his Madonna of St. Zaccaria, painted (1505) when he was already old, but to me the most wonderful of his paintings. The Madonna sits here beneath a vaulted dome, four Saints wait on her in quiet attendance, and beneath her throne a child angel plays the viol; all swims in a soft golden light, and the work must have influenced profoundly his contemporaries, and connects itself with his brilliant pupil Giorgione.

Carlo Crivelli, who may be studied at his best in our own Gallery, falls without the scope of my subject here. A supremely great decorator, though he lived and worked away from Venice he is proud to be her citizen, and signs himself " Carolus Crivellus Venetus." Of course, the Venice Academy is indispensable to our study of her art. We can trace there the development of her painting from the earliest times to the masters of her eighteenth century art : through the Bellini and their predecessors, through the pageant and legend pictures of Carpaccio and Mansueti, then the masters of the golden time, Titian, Palma Vecchio, Veronese, Bonifazio, down to Ricci, Piazzetta and Tiepolo in the later days of the old Republic. The Gallery owed much to the energy and " flair " of its Director, Giulio Cantalamessa, who died at Rome last year, and I can recollect when Palma's wonderful " Holy Conversation " was added by him to its treasures; but the present management of the Gallery under Fogolari and Giuseppe Fiocco, follows his tradition. The famous " Assumption of Madonna," once the glory of this Gallery, has found its true home again in the Church of the Frari ; and it is to the churches of Venice that we must turn to continue our study of her painters. First of all the Frari for Titian (here, too, his " Madonna of the Pesaro family ") and Bellini, and for this last-named St. Zaccaria. Then Sta. Maria Formosa for Palma Vecchio's glorious altarpiece of Sta. Barbara, S. Sebastiano for Veronese's story of Esther, S. Giovanni Crisostomo for Sebastiano del Piombo's altarpiece, with its lovely group of female Saints, S. Giovanni in Bragora for Bordone, the Madonna dell'Orto and the Scuola of S. Rocco for Tintoretto, the Church of the Gesuati, Sta. Maria del Rosario and S. Alvise for Tiepolo. Lastly, the Ducal Palace itself, a perfect treasure house of Venetian painting, illustrating the story and the grandeur of the Republic, and culminating in Veronese's magnificent " Venice enthroned " of the Sala del Maggiore Consiglio. For here Venezia, in the great ceiling painting, sits enthroned, golden-haired and with skin cool and clear as pearl, clad in silk and ermine, the sceptre of empire in her hand, the subject peoples of her rule below, while a spirit wings

11

down to set the crown upon her brow; a queenly being, Venice, the City Triumphant, painted by a master of ceremonial grandeur.

"Splendour! all cries to me here of splendour!" ("Pracht! pracht! alles schreit mir pracht!") I remember always these words spoken to me by a German friend years ago at Venice. We were just stepping into our gondola, and right before us, across the Canal rose the white splendour of Longhena's Church of the Salute. I question if the remark was entirely complimentary, for the lady was an enthusiastic Ruskinian, and all her eyes were for the old; but it seems to me just to give the true impression on a fresh mind already steeped in art. In this necessarily brief survey I have had to pass by much that is of interest in the art of Venice; but its keynote is always this glory of colour, reflected in her sunlit lagoons, brought back by her galleys from voyages of adventure in the Eastern seas—suggested already in the art of the Muranese, breaking through the quiet religious beauty of Bellini, flaming out, triumphant, in that glory of colour, that " fiammegiare dei colori " of the greatest of them all, Giorgione. It is the rare gift of certain artists—and it was his—to create a new undreamed of type of human beauty. Last month in Bridgewater House I seemed to trace this in a lovely painting there, though not placed under his name : it appears in his St. Catherine of St. Marcuola, again—reflected perhaps in Titian's art—in the figures of "Profane and Sacred Love"; and without doubt in those wonderful decorations of the Fondaco dei Tedeschi, carried through with young Titian (perhaps in that beautiful woman " like a Judith ", seen by Vasari) this new loveliness, this glory of colour carried all Venice by storm. Caught up, developed by Titian, this Giorgionesque tradition diffuses itself over the Venetian school, over Titian's no less great contemporary Jacopo Palma, over Paolo Cagliari, called Veronese, the superb master of Venetian festival, over Del Piombo, before he came to Michelangelo in Rome, over Tintoretto in his portraits, his paintings of S. Rocco, his " Last Judgment " of S. Maria dell'Orto—the souls swept down like leaves before a hurricane—his " Marriage of Bacchus and Ariadne " of the Ducal Palace, with its play of shadow over ivory flesh tones. Even the painters, like Varotari, of a later age inherit the great tradition, and hand it down to the last of the Venetian masters, Giovanni Battista Tiepolo.

At the same time Venice was drinking in all the culture of the full Renaissance. Never a city of scholarship, like Florence, she yet offered her shelter and hospitality to the scholars and the Greek exiles. In 1469 a printing press was introduced; and Nicholas Jenson was followed later by Aldus Manutius, while for two centuries Venice was a centre of printing and her book trade was immense. The beautiful glass work brought from Bohemia found an abiding home in Venice, while in

12

architecture and sculpture the Lombardi family—Pietro, in that loveliest little church of Sta. Maria dei Miracoli, his sons Antonio and, greatest of them all, Tullio, architect to the Republic—express in marble forms of wonderful charm the new spirit of the Renaissance. Their work may be studied at Padua (S. Antonio) and at Venice in the monument of Doge Mocenigo in SS. Giovanni e Paolo ; and Tullio probably had worked in this church on the Vendramin tomb with Alessandro Leopardi, that sculptor of genius who, without this same church, completed the equestrian figure of the great Venetian Condottiere, Bartolommeo Colleoni. It was Leopardi who designed for the Piazza of St. Mark the three great standard-bearers of bronze, with winged lions, sea-nymphs and Tritons : but now came to Venice the Tuscan sculptor, Jacopo Sansovino, that master of his art who for forty years was Protomastro of the Most Serene Republic. None could express better than he in stone this sense of the splendid regal beauty of Venice of his time. The friend of Titian, Veronese and Aretino, he reveals in another art the message they had given. The forceful " bravura " of his style was suited to the city and pleased the Venetian aristocracy : it is at its best in the richly ornate grandeur of the Staircase of the Giants within the Ducal Palace, in the Library of St. Mark (built in 1536), and in the exquisite bronze reliefs of his Loggetta beneath the Campanile of S. Marco.

At the same time the churches of Venice—S. Maria Gloriosa dei Frari, SS. Giovanni e Paolo, S. Salvatore, S. Maria Formosa, S. Zaccaria, S. Maria dell'Orto, S. Giovanni Crisostomo, S. Giovanni in Bragora, S. Giorgio degli Schiavoni—were being filled with splendid creations in colour or marble ; and both in the city and on the Grand Canal extended that wonderful line of Palaces, which in 1495 De Comynes had admired—the Palazzo Dario (of the Lombardi time), the Contarini Fasan, the later Corner della Cà Grande (designed in 1532 by Sansovino), the Loredan, Mocenigo, Giustiniani or Foscari (at the corner of the Canal, added to by Doge Francesco Foscari), the splendid Contarini delle Figure of the early Renaissance, like the Vendramin-Calergi and the Corner Spinelli ; while the Grimani, designed by Sanmicheli, is central Renaissance, and the Rezzonico and Pesaro Palaces carry us down to Longhena, the architect of that glorious church on this Canal—an inspiration of the Baroque spirit—Sta. Maria della Salute, which, like Palladio's church of the Redentore, is a votive church for deliverance from the plague.

Lastly, that even more beautiful creation of the Gothic art, the Palace called Cà d'Oro (1424-36), with "its maze of interwoven arches, its stone work blooming everywhere into frozen flowers "—which I found, when I was able to visit it last summer, undergoing a careful and judicious restoration. From the balcony here I could see the sweep of

13

the Canal, and could picture to myself something of the scene of those old days, when Giorgione's and Titian's frescoes were yet glowing on the walls of the Fondaco dei Tedeschi, when the Fondaco dei Turchi across the Canal was busy with merchants and all the commerce of the East, when that pageantry of Venetian splendour was at its full : such a scene of Venetian sunset as Aretino describes—" the innumerable boats filled with foreigners as well as the people of the city, giving joy not merely to the gazers but to the Grand Canal itself, that perpetual delight of all who plough its waters . . . while the buildings of Venice, though of solid stone, seemed made of some ethereal substance."

Sprung from that little group of exiles on Torcello the city had developed through the centuries into perfect life, a thing of glorious and unique beauty, a flower whose petals lay opened to the sun : yet deep within holding the germ—the fate of all beautiful human things—of future decay.

## CHAPTER III

### THE EIGHTEENTH CENTURY IN VENICE

T the close of the second chapter it was suggested that the splendour of Venice, at its height in the later years of the sixteenth century, had been more apparent than real ; that the brilliant and powerful City-State, Queen of those southern seas, held already in her bosom the certain germs of future decay. Let me now mention some of the reasons which lead us inevitably to this conclusion.

Venice had for centuries held in her grasp the trade of the East, had been the meeting place of East and West, commercially their centre of exchange. We may probably locate the highest point she attained in those nine years (1414-23) under the wise rule of Doge Mocenigo, to whom she owed the completion of her Ducal Palace : but that ruler foresaw the danger lurking for her under the pride of power, and on his death-bed he besought the Council, if they valued his advice, not to elect Francesco Foscari as his successor. He did this because he knew Foscari to be an able and ambitious man, and because he dreaded for the sea-city he loved the results of a policy of expansion on the mainland. He died, and after hesitancy, for his word carried weight, his advice was set aside, Foscari was elected ; and what he had foreseen, and even worse, in course of time ensued. Venice, with her far-seeing and firm government, her great sea-power, was an immense force, and might even have conceivably come to dominate divided Italy ; but

14

an aggressive mainland policy of expansion was bound to bring her into conflict with the Papacy—which had always opposed Italian unification—then with the Duchy of Milan, and in a less degree with Florence and Naples.

This was, in fact, exactly what happened. Foscari's acquisition of territory in north Italy led to a long and exhausting war with Filippo Maria, Duke of Milan : then, suddenly, the great danger which threatened Venice in her trade, her sea-power, her very existence, disclosed itself—and found her unprepared. In the East she had hitherto been opposed by the decadent Eastern Empire : but when the Turk appeared in Europe the whole position became changed. Byzantium was besieged, and Venice, though warned of the coming danger, found her resources exhausted, her fleet depleted ; the city of Constantine fell after heroic resistance, abandoned by Christendom, whose battle against the Turk Venice, alone, at a disadvantage, had now to fight in the Eastern seas. At the same time other causes contributed to weaken her. The discovery of the Cape route, as well as of America itself, turned aside from her quays the traffic of the world ; and the powers of Western Europe, France, Germany, Spain, who, in place of uniting against the infidel, were then quarrelling and ravaging Italy as their battle-ground, united, at the suggestion of a Pope, to destroy the power of Venice, and divide between them the spoil. If Venice saved herself in the end by the devotion of her people (even those of the mainland remained faithful at heart), yet the blow was one which left indelible traces.

With time, too, that ancient heroic spirit of the Venetian, which had sent a whole people with the cry of " S. Marco " into the pass of Malamocco, had become softened, more pleasure-loving, less virile. The nobles had ere this abandoned trade, as beneath their dignity ; and in the eighteenth century the strongest passions of the city seem to centre round the theatre, the concert, the gaming tables. In a chapter on the fall of Venice in my " City Triumphant "[1] I have analysed the social conditions of this unique city in that century, when Venice—like the old society of Europe—was approaching her end, but seemed indifferent to anything save amusement ; and those who would follow further the Venetian life of this period may study it in the pages of Monnier,[2] of Molmenti,[3] in the memoirs of the period or the inimitable Comedies of Goldoni. The forms of Government remained the same, but within all had changed. Venice of those days has been called " une île enchantée, une abbaye de Thélème," whose device is " fais

[1] V. Selwyn Brinton. " The City Triumphant." Ch. 3.
[2] V. Philippe Monnier. " Venise au XVIIIe Siècle."
[3] V. P. Molmenti. " La Vie Privée à Venise." Venice, F. Ongania, 1897.

15

ce que voudra," and where amusement is the only concern of life. Lady Montagu had written that "whoever knows Venice must agree that it is the centre of pleasure." The life of the city now centres round the Piazza, the Broglio, where the nobles meet to discuss politics or love affairs, the Ridotto, where the gaming tables are never idle, the theatres, the two hundred cafés and countless "casinos," alight till the early hours of the morning.

Music, cultivated everywhere throughout Europe, was in Venice a passion; and the concerts in the hospitals or Orphan Asylums—the Pietà, the Derelitti, the Mendicanti—where the girls, in the dress of nuns, formed the orchestra and often sang divinely, were famous throughout Europe. The theatres, opened in October, were no less frequented, and were the scene, in this age, of Goldoni's comedies, written for the Venetian public and played under the author's direction, as well as that "Teatro Fiabesco" of Carlo Gozzi, who at the Teatro S. Samuele took Venice by storm. In the summer the villas on the Brenta were filled with the Venetian nobles, who came there for their "villegiatura," and brought into the repose of the country their brilliant and artificial surroundings; while private life had arrived at a freedom which did not exist elsewhere. The position of women, which, in the old Republic, had kept the sex apart from public affairs and in an almost Oriental seclusion, had now entirely changed. No married woman was in the "mode" without possessing her "cavaliere servente" or "cicisbeo," who existed for her amusement, attended her from morning till night, privileged even to assist in the lengthy mysteries of her toilet: the husband, ceding willingly his position, would have considered it bad taste to interfere, or was himself busied in the same relations with some other fair one. Carnovale lasted for six months in the year, and the whole city went masked, "whether priest or layman"—writes De Brosses in his memoirs—"even the Papal Nuncio and the Prior of the Capucins": with the "baútta," the mantle of black silk, and the half-mask over the face—as we see them in the paintings of Longhi or Guardi—the disguise was complete, and the Venetian of either sex, from the patrician to the "tabarro," the man of the people, could go forth in search of adventure with impunity. Even the nuns thus disguised (for the convents had become notoriously lax) could take their part in the follies of Carnovale, wander at night through the enchanted city, or in the daytime receive their friends and admirers within the "parlatorio" of the convent. "Venice in those days"—I have said elsewhere—"had become the pleasure ground of Europe; where all ranks, all classes of society—even the convents, as we have seen, were not excepted—joined in the universal scramble for amusement."

16

Yet amid all this the banner of St. Mark still floated over Venice and her subject cities, the form of the great Republic, the "Serenissima," remained unchanged. Alone in Italy Venice remained unconquered by the alien, had stood beside Mantua in her hour of agony against the Imperialists, had held their own against the Spanish domination; and now, out of this strange fantastic life of pleasure, there comes to bloom a new art which has its own fascination. For here, in this still free soil, the great tradition had never quite died out. Alessandro Varotari, called Padovanino, who may be best studied in the Venice Academy, is a successor to the grand style of Veronese; and, though the age he lived in, with Contarini and others, was one of decline, very early in the eighteenth century begins a new movement.

In our time Guardi, Longhi, Tiepolo, hold their own against the best; but we must go back farther to reach their precursors. Only in late years the art of the Sei-Cento is beginning to be better understood; and Giovanni Battista Piazzetta had been influenced no doubt, when at Bologna, by the work of the Caracci, of Crespi, and that master of light and shade, Guercino. A masterpiece of his art is "L'Indovina" (Venice Academy), where the buxom figure of a country wench bathed in full sunlight is from his strong brush, and where are also his drawings. Around him a whole group of artists come to share in this movement. It is for them, too—as for Goldoni's delightful Venetian in "Pamela" —an age of travel; and some Venetian painters, finding the English good patrons, came as far as London, among them Sebastiano Ricci with his nephew Marco, both of whom came to influence the art in Venice of their time. And the vogue of the time was for the "picturesque"—classic ruins, buildings, landscapes and figures—for which there was a strong demand, especially among the foreign visitors, supplied very efficiently by such painters as Marieschi, Zuccarelli, or Zais.

But here we come to touch on two masters who belong not only to their age, but to all time. Antonio Canale, born in Venice (1697), went to Rome to paint her ruins; then, returning to Venice, gave himself to the beauty of her palaces and lagoons. He had numerous commissions from Mr. Joseph Smith, the British Consul at Venice (1752-1760), who was buying pictures for the Royal Collection, and in fact there are still many of Canaletto's paintings at Windsor: the artist himself visited England and spent two years, or more, painting, till our climate drove him back to the lagoons. His paintings of Venice, admirable in drawing and perspective, and often in colour (as in his "Grand Canal with S. Simone" of the Wallace Collection) in their own field cannot be surpassed. He gives us the Venice that we know, faithfully, if sometimes coldly, rendered: he found his place at once and held it, while

17

it has taken almost a hundred years for Guardi to come into his own.

There seems no doubt, from the results of recent research—and here the names of Gino Fogolari and Giuseppe Fiocco of the Venice Academy are to be mentioned with gratitude—that Francesco Guardi had commenced with his brother Antonio as a figure painter, and that the story—in Gradenigo's diary of 1764—of his being a good pupil of the famous Canaletto must be considered open to question. He remains, indeed, always a good figure artist; but it is his landscape, his marvellous " capricci," his paintings of Venice which hold us now. He loves to depict the Piazza, the Piazzetta, or the Grand Canal alive with figures, or with swiftly moving gondolas (as in his " Dogana " of our Wallace Collection) : for the human interest in his work is as strong as is the wonderful sense of atmosphere. Simonson says very justly of this latter point that " what strikes one in Guardi's views of Venice is the attention which he paid to effects of light and atmosphere : such sparkling effects as he has produced are not to be found in Canale's pictures." Symonds has remarked, no less truly, in his essay on Longhi, that " Canaletto filled large canvases with mathematical perspectives of city and water, at the same time he omitted life and incident. There is little to remind us that the Venice he so laboriously depicted was the Venice of perukes and bag wigs, of masks and hoops and Carnival disguises. Guardi had an eye for local and fashionable humours. The result is that some of his small pictures (one, for instance, which represents a brilliant reception in the Sala del Collegio of the Ducal Palace) have a real value for us in recalling the life of a vanished and irrevocable past."

For both Guardi and his contemporary Pietro Longhi loved to paint the Carnovale of Venice with its costume and disguises—the mask and " baútta " worn by both sexes, the Zendaletto of the women, the Senators in their long robes and full wigs; it has been even questioned as to which of these two painted those brilliant scenes of the Masquerade in the Ridotto and the " Parlatorio " of S. Zaccaria ; and the balance seems to turn in favour of Longhi, though Guardi was a fine enough figure artist to have drawn that clever group of masks. He is at his best in his " Capricci," which many prefer even to his paintings, picturesque improvisations of nature, sparkling with life and in which his nervous brush or crayon (he used sepia freely in these drawings) finds free expression ; and which may be studied, like the paintings just mentioned, in the Museo Correr. In his paintings, after the canvas was covered, he seems to have used touches of more solid impasto (*réhauts*) to accentuate, and impart the brilliancy and movement he loved ; but he paints temperamentally, and his technique varies with his mood and subject.

18

Lastly—and perhaps greatest of all these later men—we come to Giovanni Battista Tiepolo; born at Venice, in the people's quarter, he studied under Lazzarini, and at twenty-three married Cecilia, the sister of Francesco Guardi. Sig. Fiocco,[1] in his work on Guardi, mentions the influence of Alessandro Magnasco on these later Venetians; and an exhibition arranged in London by the Magnasco Society seems to confirm this in the case of both Ricci and Tiepolo. But Tiepolo stands alone, unsurpassed in his art. More theatrical than Veronese (for he lived in an artificial age) he plays with his colour (I have said of him) " as a great musician with harmonies of sound "—he loves to fill great spaces of wall or ceiling with triumphant figures of colour, with radiant dreams of heavenly glory, or the pageantry of earthly splendour; he fills the churches of Venice (the Gesuati, S. Alvise, Sta. Maria della Pieta, S. Filippo, the Scuola Oel Carmine), and the palaces of the city and the neighbouring mainland (Palazzo Ducale, Palazzo Labia, Palazzo Rezzonico, Palazzo Martinengo Michiel, Villa Pisani at Strà, Villa Valmarana near Vicenza) with his stupendous creations. Invited to Spain (where I admired his frescoes in the Royal Palace of Madrid) he died there in 1770.

And now the shadow of her doom had come very near to this brilliant pleasure house of Europe, which Venice had in these years become. Ere the century was out the armies of the French Republic, led by young Buonaparte in the flush of his first victories, were to invade Italy and threaten the still free city of the lagoons. On May 1st of 1797 the French leader declared war on Venice. " I will have none of your alliance,"—he said—" none of your Senate, of your Inquisitors. I will be a second Attila to Venice." The city had no force to oppose his advance: on May 12th of that year the ancient Republic had ceased to exist.

## CHAPTER IV

## VENICE OF THE PRESENT

UT Venice had never really died. When she was trampled on by Buonaparte, handed over, like a tame or dead thing, at Campo Formio to Austria, held for half a century under the alien, the old spirit was still there, ready to flame out when there came the hope of better days; and when the new message of the nation made one, of " Italia Unita," spread through the peninsula, from Naples of the Bourbons to Milan beneath the Hapsburg, it found nowhere a warmer or more

[1] Giuseppe Fiocco. " Francesco Guardi," page 43.

passionate welcome, a more heroic spirit of sacrifice than in the city of the lagoons, heir to the tradition of thirteen centuries of glorious freedom. In 1848 the Venetians rose in arms, and in the Piazza called for liberty of Tommaseo and Manin, imprisoned by the Austrians : the Republic was proclaimed, with Manin as its President, and, though the city was forced back into servitude after seventeen months of single-handed and heroic resistance, in 1861 Venice became an integral part of that Kingdom.

At the same time, with her recovery of political existence, there had come to Venice the waking of a new and modern spirit in her art. When the "Serenissima" had perished beneath the soldiers of Buonaparte the city, like all Italy, had been invaded by new art and fashions. To those creations of Guardi or Tiepolo, to the portraits of Longhi or Rosalba Carriera had succeeded the paintings of Appiano, Sabatelli or Camuccini, the sculpture of Canova : within the home dress, decoration followed suit, and the charming creations of Andrea Brustolon gave place to the coldly classic furniture of the "Style Empire." The art of Venice centred in the Academy, then transferred to the Convent of the Carità, where the young Heyez had studied before he went to Rome to seek the inspiration and counsel of Canova ; and thence to work in Milan, where, in the middle of the century Mosé Bianchi, Tranquillo Cremona (born also in Venice, but coming from thence to Milan) and Filippo Carcano (that veteran of art, whom it was my privilege to know before he passed away) were seeking to bring back reality to art.

But in Venice herself the influence of the city in her past, her unique charm, became a predominant element in art creation. That tradition of her individual beauty, inherited from the scenes of pageant of Bellini or Carpaccio, detailed by Canale, revealed in all its radiance by Guardi, became the cult of a succession of artists up to even our own time, who seek, like the two masters just mentioned, to give us Venice—"Venice, asleep like a miracle of opal or of pearl," but, at the same time, "the true Venice, a little grey, bathed in an atmosphere of silver."[1] We trace back these beginnings of her new art to Cabianca, but, above all to Giacomo Favretto, who, in his "Liston," the last of his paintings shown at Venice in 1887, seeks his inspiration (like Emma Ciardi or Italico Brass in our day) in the Venice of the eighteenth century, that age of periwigs and courtly intrigue : but elsewhere ("Il Traghetto," "Ponte di Rialto" and other paintings) gives us a fresh and direct impression of the Venice that we know. In the same Exhibition of 1887, when Favretto came for the last time before the public, appeared Luigi Nono, Ettore Tito, Gugliemo Ciardi, Bressanin,

[1] P. Molmenti. "La Pittura Veneziana."

20

Fragiacomo—whose recent loss we deplore—Cesare Laurenti, painter, sculptor and architect, Angelo dal Oca Bianca, Alessandro Milesi—names which have appeared in the succeeding Venice Exhibitions as representative of the best in modern Venetian art.

Professore Ettore Tito, whose work I have been privileged to analyse and illustrate in the pages of "The Studio," is a fine draughtsman, a great decorator, somewhat in the old Venetian tradition of Tiepolo, a portraitist of merit—but even more attractive in another side of his art. Born at Castellamare, in 1859, he came when still young to Venice, and drank deep of her peculiar fascination. No painter has excelled him in those scenes of Venetian popular life—"Peschiera," "Laguna," "La Gomena," "Sul Murazzo," "Chioggia,"—where the figures of the boys and fishermen, the slim lithe forms of the women are alive, and bring into the canvas the fresh clean air of the lagoons. In recent years Professore Tito has been head of the schools of the Venice Academy. Gugliemo Ciardi took Venice and the Veneto for his subject, and treated this theme with masterly technique and fine perception : the Ciardi, living in S. Barnaba, are a family of artists, and, when Gugliemo passed away but recently, he left a worthy successor to his art in his son Beppe Ciardi, while the latter's sister, Emma Ciardi, apart from her paintings of modern Venice, has treated the life there of the eighteenth century with distinction and charm. A recent loss to Venice is that of Marius Pictor, a painter of great imaginative power, some of whose work we here illustrate.

Meanwhile the city has grown and prospered, and the new harbour works, when completed, without interfering with her picturesque beauty will enable Venice to vie with Trieste as one of the chief seaports of the Adriatic. Her glass work and mosaic—a heritage of earlier days—still find a market, with velvet and silk ; and trade is also done in grain and wine, spirits, fish, hides and leather. But above all Venice, with her beauty of the past and her sea charm, is still the haunt of most artists with anything in them of romance and imagination. They come from every part of the world, each contributing something of his own personality. The idle swarming crowds, which the native Venetian artist of the eighteenth century shows, give place to the lonely grandeurs which Turner saw. We illustrate here the work of artists from America, France, Germany, England, and the work also of modern Italian artists. The variety of their points of view contributes to the unity of the general impression. Monet gives us the misty haze which Turner aimed at. Brangwyn recalls the sumptuous pageant of the fifteenth century. We have etchers like Sir D. Y. Cameron and Sir Charles Holroyd, who set down in the essential delicacy of their medium the fine lines of architectural detail. Zorn with his northern realism gives

21

us a picture of actual work in his " Lace Makers, Venice." If there is a distinction between the modern Italian and the foreign artist it is that the former is concerned with its present life, the latter with its tradition and its buildings. Ettore Tito will paint the Fish Market, or the Canal with the busy little motor boats that ply to and fro ; Carbonati, the people that throng the streets. Sargent, on the other hand, is interested in the great buildings which he records with the swift certainty of water-colour. It is perhaps natural that the foreigner should see the past and the native artist the present. In the brilliant and successful series of International Art Exhibitions, arranged biennially within the Public Gardens by the City of Venice, both these expressions of Venice have found their appropriate place.

In this new Italy, an united progressive nation, the Republic of the " Serenissima " could have no place. But Venice herself remains a city and home of art—for that runs in her very life blood—a watch-tower of Italy, looking northward to the Alps and eastward to the sea— who had faced without flinching the storm and terror of the Great War . . . a jewel—perhaps the greatest jewel—in that diadem of her ancient and world-famed cities set around the brows of an united Italy.

22

# THE INSPIRATION OF VENICE TO ART

Tercia etas mundi

Tercia etas mundi     Foliñ . XLIIII

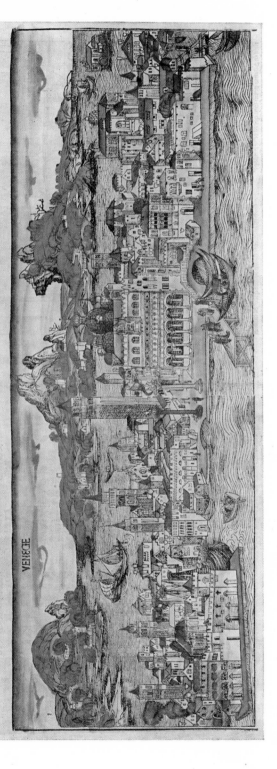

VENECE

VENICE IN 1493. COLOURED WOODCUT
FROM THE NÜREMBERG CHRONICLE.

*Macpherson Collection.*

In the Bodleian Library, Oxford.

VENICE IN THE TIME OF MARCO POLO. XIVᴛʜ CENTURY MS.

26

COURTYARD OF A VENETIAN PALACE. XVITH CENTURY ITALIAN PAINTING.

*In the Victoria and Albert Museum.*

VENICE IN 1502. GERMAN WOODCUT.

*Macpherson Collection.*

27

THE MIRACLE OF THE HOLY CROSS. BY GENTILE BELLINI.

*In the Academy, Venice.*

29

*In the Doge's Palace.*

THE DOGE RECEIVING THE SWORD OF
ALEXANDER III. BY LEANDRO BASSANO.

30

*Septentrio*

PALATII SENATORII APVD VENETOS CONFLAGRATIO,
ANNO M D LXXVII.

THE BURNING OF THE DOGE'S PALACE, 1578.
LINE ENGRAVING BY GEORG HOUFNAGEL.

In the *Prado Museum, Madrid.*

THE COUNCIL CHAMBER.   BY PIETRO MALOMBRA.

33

34

*In the Prado Museum, Madrid.*

VENICE FROM THE SALUTE.  BY LEANDRO BASSANO.

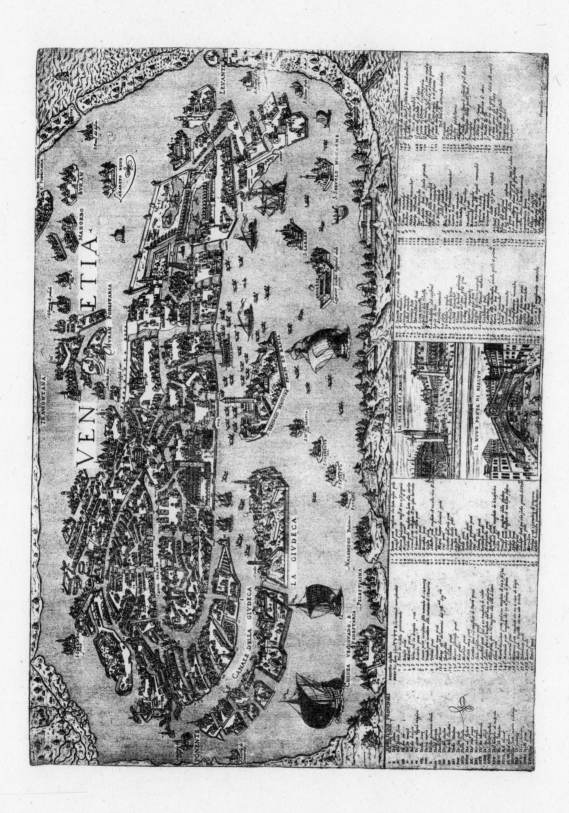

PLAN OF VENICE, c. 1590. LINE ENGRAVING.

*Macpherson Collection.*

35

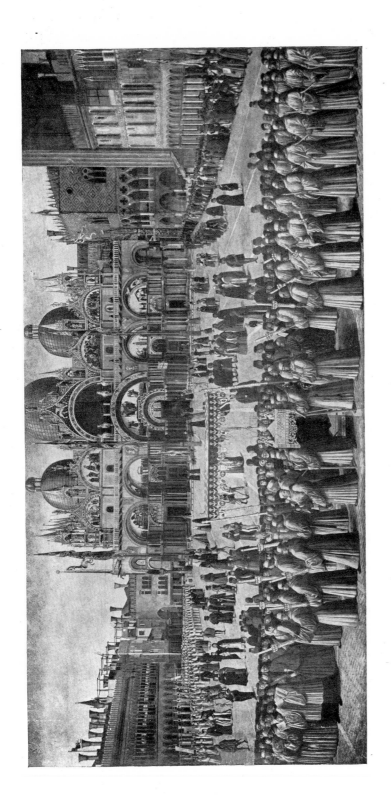

PROCESSION TO ST. MARK'S.   BY GENTILE BELLINI.

*In the Academy, Venice.*

37

In the Dresden Gallery.        THE DOGE LOREDANO.  BY GIOVANNI BELLINI.

38

*Macpherson Collection.*

ST. MARK'S IN THE XVITH CENTURY.
LINE ENGRAVING BY GEORG HOUFNAGEL.

*In the Academy, Venice.*

FISHERMAN HANDING THE RING TO THE
DOGE GRADENIGO.  BY PARIS BORDONE.

41

42

VENICE IN THE EARLY XVIIITH CENTURY. LINE ENGRAVING BY PETER SCHENK.

*Macpherson Collection.*

*Macpherson Collection.*

VIEW OF THE DOGANA, 1702.    LINE ENGRAVING BY PETER SCHENK.

43

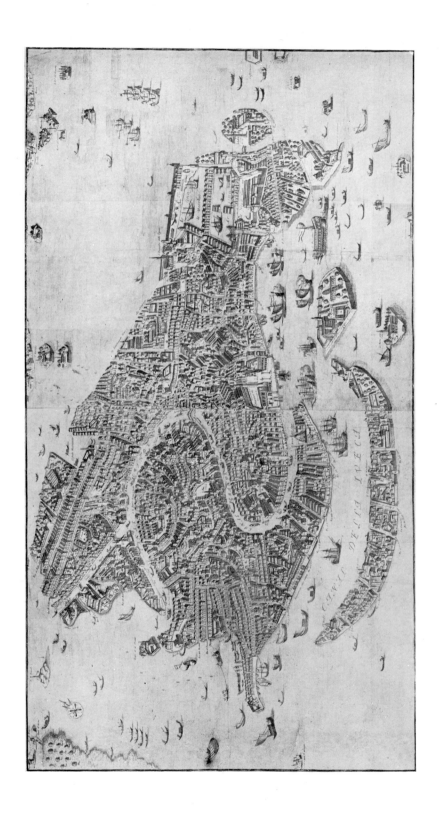

*Macpherson Collection.*

PLAN OF VENICE, c 1700.   LINE ENGRAVING.

*In the possession of Sir Robert Witt.*

VIEW OF VENICE.  PEN AND WASH DRAWING BY ABRAHAM STORCK.

45

46

*In the Prado Museum, Madrid.*

VIEW OF VENICE WITH THE DOGE'S PALACE.   BY KASPAR VAN WITTEL (VAN VITELLI).

THE COURTYARD, DOGE'S PALACE, WITH THE PROCESSION
OF THE PAPAL LEGATE.    BY ANTONIO CANALETTO.

*In the possession of Messrs. Tooth and Sons, Ltd.*

47

48

A FÊTE DAY, VENICE.  BY ANTONIO CANALETTO.

*In the possession of Messrs. Tooth and Sons, Ltd.*

*In the Pinacoteca, Venice.*

THE SCUOLA DI S. MARCO.   BY ANTONIO CANALETTO.

50

THE GRAND CANAL.  BY ANTONIO CANALETTO.

*In the Frankfort Gallery.*

RECEPTION OF COUNT GERGI AT VENICE.    BY ANTONIO CANALETTO.

*In the Hermitage, Petrograd.*

51

THE FOUR HORSES OF ST. MARK'S.  BY ANTONIO CANALETTO.

SCENE ON THE GRAND CANAL.   SCHOOL OF CANALETTO.

REPAIRING THE CAMPANILE. PEN AND
WASH DRAWING BY ANTONIO CANALETTO.

VIEWS OF VENICE IN THE XVIITH
CENTURY. BY JOHAN RICHTER.

56

VENETIAN RECEPTION. BY PIETRO LONGHI.

RECEPTION OF THE GRAND DUKE AND DUCHESS OF
RUSSIA, 1782. LINE ENGRAVING BY ANTONIO BARATTI.

57

*In the possession of H. Yates Thompson, Esq.*

CHURCH OF THE FRARI. PAINTING BY MICHELE MARIESCHI.

59

60

*By permission of Max Rothschild, Esq.*

THE BUCENTAUR LEAVING FOR THE LIDO. BY FRANCESCO GUARDI.

CHURCH OF THE REDENTORE. BY FRANCESCO GUARDI.

*By permission of Max Rothschild, Esq.*

61

62

ANTECHAMBER OF THE DOGE'S PALACE. BY FRANCESCO GUARDI.

*In the possession of Sr. Mario Crespi.*

In the Wallace Collection.

SANTA MARIA DELLA SALUTE. BY FRANCESCO GUARDI.

PROCESSION OF THE DOGE TO S. ZACCARIA. BY FRANCESCO GUARDI.

FÊTE OF CORPUS DOMINI.  BY FRANCESCO GUARDI.

*In the Louvre, Paris.*

66

DOGE EMBARKING ON THE BUCENTAUR. BY FRANCESCO GUARDI.

*In the Louvre, Paris.*

67

68

FÊTE OF MAUNDY THURSDAY. BY FRANCESCO GUARDI.

*In the Louvre, Paris*

POPE PIUS VI BLESSING THE VENETIAN
PEOPLE. BY FRANCESCO GUARDI.

*By permission of the Visitors of the Ashmolean Museum, Oxford.*

69

By permission of Max Rothschild, Esq.

DOGANA WITH WOODEN BRIDGE. BY LUCA CARLEVARIS.

VIEW OF VENICE. BY RICHARD PARKES BONINGTON.

*In the Louvre, Paris.*

71

SOUVENIR DE VENISE.   BY JAMES HOLLAND.

VIEW ON THE GRAND CANAL.
BY RICHARD PARKES BONINGTON.

THE RIALTO.  WATER-COLOUR DRAWING BY GIACOMO GUARDI.

*In the possession of Sir Robert Witt.*

76

THE DOGANA. LINE ENGRAVING BY EDWARD
A. GOODALL AFTER CLARKSON STANFIELD, R.A.

*In the British Museum.*

In the Victoria and Albert Museum.

VENICE.   WATER-COLOUR  DRAWING  BY  W.  J.  MÜLLER.

77

78

SAN PIETRO DE CASTELLO.  LINE ENGRAVING BY
R. WALLIS,  AFTER  CLARKSON  STANFIELD,  R.A.

*In the British Museum.*

IN THE GULF OF VENICE.   LINE ENGRAVING BY R. WALLIS
AFTER CLARKSON STANFIELD, R.A.

*In the British Museum.*

80

VENICE. LINE ENGRAVING BY J. COUSENS AFTER CLARKSON STANFIELD, R.A.

VUE DU QUAI DES ESCLAVONS. BY J. B. C. COROT.

*Selected for purchase by the Felton Bequest Trustees*
*for the National Gallery of Victoria, Melbourne.*

81

82

THE APPROACH TO VENICE. BY J. M. W. TURNER, R.A.

In the Tate Gallery.

In the National Gallery.

THE "SUN OF VENICE" GOING TO SEA.  BY J. M. W. TURNER, R.A.

85

86

VENICE FROM THE GIUDECCA.   BY J. M. W. TURNER, R.A.

*In the City of Leicester Art Gallery.*

VENICE—CANALETTI PAINTING BY J. M. W. TURNER, R.A.

*In the Tate Gallery.*

In the Victoria and Albert Museum.

VENICE. BY J. M. W. TURNER, R.A.

89

THE MARRIAGE OF THE ADRIATIC.  BY J. M. W. TURNER, R.A.

TWO VIEWS OF VENICE. LITHOGRAPHS BY
J. D. HARDING AFTER R. P. BONINGTON.

INTERIOR OF ST. MARK'S.   DRAWING BY SAMUEL PROUT.

CÀ D'ORO.   DRAWING BY SAMUEL PROUT.

94

ABOVE: PALAZZO MOCENIGO.   BELOW: THE RIALTO.
LINE ENGRAVINGS BY R. WALLIS AFTER S. PROUT.

DETAIL OF ST. MARK'S.   WASH DRAWING BY JOHN RUSKIN.

97

VENICE IN 1848—WAR. BY MARIUS PICTOR.

VENICE IN 1848—HUNGER.  BY MARIUS PICTOR.

VENICE IN 1848—PLAGUE.  BY MARIUS PICTOR.

100

S. GIORGIO MAGGIORE BY MOONLIGHT.   BY EDWARD A. GOODALL, R.W.S.

101

THE PUBLIC GARDENS AT VENICE. BY FÉLIX ZIEM.

FACADE OF ST. MARK'S.   BY FÉLIX ZIEM.

ON THE GRAND CANAL.  BY FÉLIX ZIEM.

FISHING BOATS ON THE ADRIATIC.  BY FÉLIX ZIEM.

105

RIVA DEI SCHIAVONI. BY FÉLIX ZIEM.

106

THE RIVA (No. 1). ETCHING BY JAMES McNEILL WHISTLER.

THE LITTLE MAST.  ETCHING
BY JAMES McNEILL WHISTLER.

THE BALCONY.   ETCHING
BY JAMES McNEILL WHISTLER.

NOCTURNE : PALACES.   ETCHING BY JAMES McNEILL WHISTLER.

FLOWER MARKET, VENICE. PEN
DRAWING BY JOSEPH PENNELL.

111

BOAT BUILDING, VENICE. PEN
DRAWING BY JOSEPH PENNELL.

*In the possession of Axel Jacobsen, Esq.*  LACE-MAKERS, VENICE.  BY ANDERS ZORN.

GONDOLIERS. BY ANDERS ZORN.

*In the possession of Herman Lamm, Esq.*

116

In the *Luxembourg Museum.*

A BURIAL AT VENICE.   BY J. ST. GERMIER.

117

118

RIO DI SAN TROVASO. WATER-COLOUR DRAWING BY FRANK BRANGWYN, R.A.

*In the collection of P. A. Cohen, Esq.*

EVENING FESTA.    WATER-COLOUR BY FRANK BRANGWYN, R.A.

*In the possession of H. B. Burney, Esq.*

PONTE DELLA PAGLIA.
BY FRANK BRANGWYN, R.A.

In the collection of Miss Margaret Harwood.

TORCELLO GARDENS.   WATER-COLOUR DRAWING BY FRANK BRANGWYN, R.A.

By courtesy of Barbizon House.

THE THREE-ARCHED BRIDGE. BY FRANK BRANGWYN, R.A.

PONTE DEL PARADISO. WATER-COLOUR
DRAWING BY FRANK BRANGWYN, R.A.

THE DEPARTURE FOR THE WEDDING.
BY FRANK BRANGWYN, R.A.

In the collection of H. S. Osler, Esq., K.C., Toronto.

THE ISLAND OF S. GIORGIO MAGGIORE. BY CLAUDE MONET.

THE DOGE'S PALACE.   BY  H. B.  BRABAZON.

*In the possession of  J. S. Sargent, Esq., R.A.*

128

In the Brooklyn Museum.

SANTA MARIA DELLA SALUTE.    WATER-COLOUR DRAWING BY J. S. SARGENT, R.A.

129

130

THE BRIDGE OF SIGHS. WATER-COLOUR DRAWING, BY J. S. SARGENT, R.A.

*In the Brooklyn Museum.*

THE PIAZZETTA.   WATER-COLOUR DRAWING BY J. S. SARGENT, R.A.

*In the Brooklyn Museum.*

131

VENETIAN TAVERN.  BY  J. S. SARGENT,  R.A.

GONDOLAS BY THE PIAZZETTA. WATER-
COLOUR DRAWING BY J. S. SARGENT, R.A.

*In the Tate Gallery.*

CHIESA DELLA BRAZORA.  BY PIERRE BESRODNY.

135

SAINT MARKS VENICE  D Y CAMERON

In the British Museum.

INTERIOR OF ST. MARK'S.   ETCHING
BY SIR D. Y. CAMERON, R.A.

THE RIALTO. ETCHING BY
SIR D. Y. CAMERON, R.A.

*In the possession of Campbell Dodgson, Esq., C.B.E.*

CALLE DELLA DONNA. ETCHING BY
SIR D. Y. CAMERON, R.A.

TINTORETTO'S HOUSE.  ETCHING
BY SIR D. Y. CAMERON, R.A.

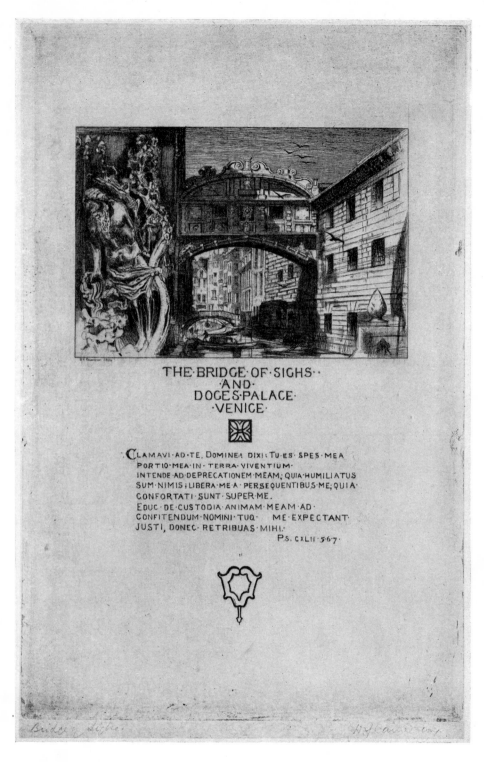

THE BRIDGE OF SIGHS. ETCHING BY
SIR D. Y. CAMERON, R.A.

CAFÉ FLORIAN.  BY ITALICO BRASS.

142

TORCELLO CATHEDRAL. LITHOGRAPH
BY WILHELM KIMBEL.

143

ST. MARK'S.  ETCHING BY WILLIAM WALCOT, R.B.A.

THE PIAZZETTA. BY WILLIAM WALCOT, R.B.A.

146

VENICE. AQUATINT BY WILLIAM WALCOT, R.B.A.

147

FLOOD IN THE PIAZZA. BY ITALICO BRASS.

149

IN THE BASIN OF ST. MARK'S. BY ETTORE TITO.

150

VENETIAN STREET STALL.  PASTEL BY H. DAVIS RICHTER, R.B.A.

151

SCENARIO.   BY   BEPPE   CIARDI.

SANTA MARIA DELLA SALUTE.  ETCHING
BY SIR CHARLES HOLROYD, R.E.

SPADARIA. LITHOGRAPH
BY ANTONIO CARBONATI.

*In the possession of Messrs. P. & D. Colnaghi and Co.*

SAN BARNABA. ETCHING BY SIR CHARLES HOLROYD, R.E.

158

RIO SAN GREGORIO.   ETCHING BY SIR CHARLES HOLROYD, R.E.

In the possession of Messrs. P. & D. Colnaghi and Co.

THE SALUTE FROM SAN GIORGIO.   BY CHARLES OPPENHEIMER, R.S.W.

159

VENETIAN PALACE. PEN AND WASH DRAWING BY MARESCO PEARCE.

GRAND CANAL, MOONLIGHT. COLOUR
WOODCUT BY YOSHIJIRO URUSHIBARA.

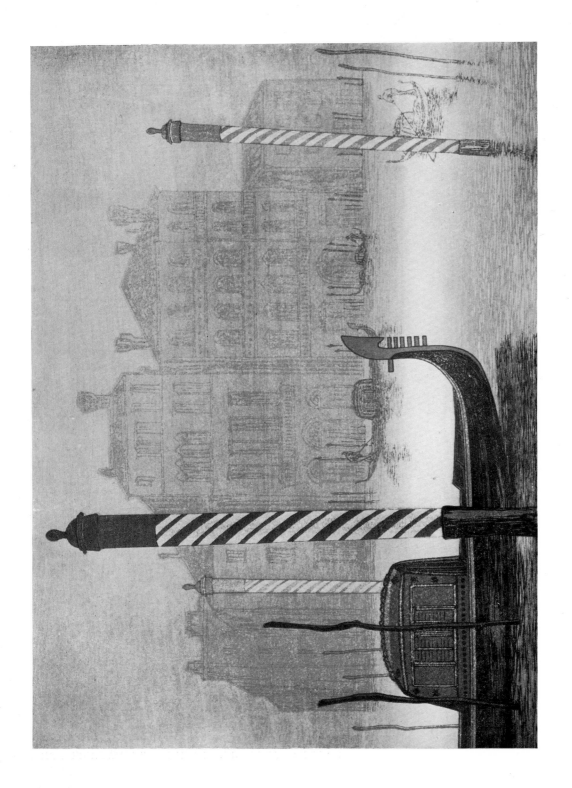

In the British Museum.

MISTY MORNING, VENICE. COLOUR WOODCUT BY YOSHIJIRO URUSHIBARA.

163

PONTE S. APOSTOLI.   ETCHING BY MAURICE ACHENER.

CANAL, CHIOGGIA.   WATER-COLOUR DRAWING BY JAMES McBEY.

THE RIVA. BY JAMES McBEY.

FAÇADE OF ST. MARK'S.  PENCIL DRAWING BY WILLIAM MONK, R.E.

SAN GIORGIO.   DRAWING BY JAMES McBEY.

169

SAN GIORGIO—SUNRISE.    BY   JAMES  McBEY.

170

SANTA MARIA FORMOSA. ETCHING BY D. S. MACLAUGHLAN.

171

THE SALUTE.  BY JAMES McBEY.

173

THE CLOCK TOWER. ETCHING
BY D. S. MACLAUGHLAN.

174

*In the British Museum.*   CALLE CROSERA.  ETCHING BY SYDNEY VACHER.

PROCESSION TO THE SALUTE.
ETCHING BY E. M. SYNGE.

RIO SAN BARNABA.  BY MAURICE BOMPARD.

ABOVE: VENETIAN SHRINE.  BELOW: LOBSTER POTS.
WATER-COLOUR DRAWINGS BY BRIDGET KEIR.

178

# THE INSPIRATION OF VENICE TO LITERATURE

Republic (*diese biberre Republik*). So that now, thank God, Venice is no more to me a mere word, an empty name, which has so often tormented me, enemy as I am of mere verbal sounds." He is lodged at " The Queen of England " near the Piazza St. Marco, and looks from his windows on a typically Venetian scene, " a narrow canal between high houses, right beneath me a single arched bridge, and opposite a small busily alive street." He is soon visiting the city, the Rialto, the Palladian churches of the Carità and Redentore. He hears the gondoliers chaunt the verses of Tasso and Ariosto to melodies of their own ; and at the " Mendicanti " can hear the oratorio of " Saul " sung by the nuns behind a grating—" the music very beautiful, the voices magnificent . . . the performance of great enjoyment, if the accursed Maestro di Capella had not beaten time with a roll of music against the grating." This part of his visit, as well as his account of the Venetian comedy, is of exceptional interest ; and may perhaps have suggested to George Sand the first chapters of her wonderful romance of " Consuelo," which first attracted me to this Venice of the eighteenth century.

The story commences, in fact, in the atmosphere of this art of music, which is the soul of Venice of that age. An oratorio is in rehearsal in the convent ; and Consuelo, a Spanish novice, is called upon by the Maestro to sing the " Salve Regina " of Pergolese. The scene is in that very church of the Mendicanti, where the great Maestro Porpora is preparing his oratorio to be given on the following Sunday of Assumption : just such a scene as Goethe, or earlier yet De Brosses, has described, where the whole concert was composed of some forty of the nuns, who " sing like angels, play the violin, the flute, the violincello, the bassoon—in a word even the largest instruments don't frighten these young ladies." Consuelo achieves her task to the delighted satisfaction of the Maestro, and to the jealousy of her fellow " jeunes choristes " ; and the love story follows, developing within this world of music, and ending, in its Venetian phase (to me the most interesting), with the sudden flight of the heroine from the city of the lagoons.

Later than Goethe came Byron, who knew Venice intimately and felt her inspiration. It was at Venice, in April of 1819, that he met the beautiful Countess Guiccioli, who had a profound, and, in many ways, a good influence in his Italian life. It was Venice who inspired, from a tragic page in her history, his " Marino Faliero, Doge of Venice," and in lighter mood that delightful improvisation of " Beppo," said to have been finished at a single sitting, as well as some of the best stanzas of " Childe Harold's Pilgrimage." Byron, it must be remembered, saw Venice in a period of political depression, and expresses this fact in his verses, notably in his not very successful " Ode on Venice," redeemed by its first lines :

182

"Oh Venice! Venice! when thy marble walls
Are level with the waters, there shall be
A cry of nations o'er thy sunken halls,
A loud lament along the sweeping sea!"
It may have been a ride with Byron along the sands of Lido, where
"The winds drove
The living spray along the sunny air
Into our faces; the blue heavens were bare
Stripped to their depths. . . ."
which inspired Shelley's delightful "Julian and Maddolo, a Conversation," with its description of a sunset on the return across the lagoons,
"As if the earth and sea had been
Dissolved into one lake of fire. . . ."
which is, to my mind, unequalled in English verse, and has been said to strike the key-note of Venetian painting.

Later in the century come the prose writers, of whom John Ruskin, with his "Stones of Venice," claims for our study a first place. He has profound sympathy with his subject, especially in the case of the earlier work, and knowledge combined with matchless English; even his denunciations of the Renaissance workers are sometimes (by no means always) not undeserved, especially when the later Baroque developed at Venice eccentricities of its own. Looking at this Renaissance period from a wider standpoint the pages of John Addington Symonds on Venetian art and story are most useful; and within our own time the researches of Pompeo Molmenti—published at Venice by Ongania, in French and Italian, under the title of "La Vie Privée à Venise," and translated recently into English by Mr. Horatio Brown, who has identified himself with the life of Venice—are a priceless contribution, covering the whole field of social life and manners from the Middle Ages to the last days of the Most Serene Republic.

Lastly, I would give a few words of appreciation to the prose and verse of the French writer, Henri de Regnier, whose "Esquisses Venitiennes," though light in touch, strikes just the right key. He comes to his subject with sympathy and appreciation:
"Sur l'eau verte, bleue ou grise
Des Canaux et du Canal,
Nous avons couru Venise
De Saint Marc à l'Arsenal
*    *    *

La gondole nous balance
Sous le felze, et, de sa main,
Le fer coupe le silence
Qui dormait dans l'air marin."

183

Venice, he tells us, is not only a city of marble and water. "She has her gardens, whose closed-in greenery holds for us something strangely rare and unexpected. Discreet and mysterious, sheltered behind their walls, they only leave to our sight the topmost branches, or the point of some cypress." Among those he selects for mention are the "Incurabili" on the Zattere, the Vendramin garden, "qui regarde le Grand Canal à travers sa porte grillée," and those of the Venier and Dario Palaces: while I recollect myself last summer crossing the Giudecca to visit a garden of wonderful beauty and extent belonging to Mrs. Eden.

Or again, coming to the Zattere by Rio S. Trovaso, he watches the great spacious tide of water looking towards the Giudecca, and drinks in the strong salt air. "I hear the midday gun. . . . The bells ring out. I have recognised those of the Gesuati, of S. Trovaso, of the Salute; now those of the Redentore, of Sta. Eufemia and of the Zitelle come to join them across the water, and the air is resonant with sound." Or yet again, the Ridotto recalls to him the Venice of Casanova and of Carlo Gozzi; or Harlequin, "avec son habit quadrillé qui lève sa batte," and his fellow comedians of the old Comedy of Art. One cannot help regretting that here, with his finished art, he has not added a pen picture (for his "Bettine" is of another race) of the "popolane," the Venetian women of the people. Were I a poet, with Regnier's gift for daintily turning verse, I might here find my inspiration. For they are a type apart, these "popolane," as distinctive as the "Madrilena," and even more refined, with something of the tradition of a great race in their carriage. The black shawls (white in the days of Longhi and Guardi) suit them admirably—and they know it. They must be of good material and cost good money, as my Venetian model told me one summer, when I had a studio on the Zattere. There are fashions in these shawls, for last summer I seemed to note fringes had lengthened; and they need the neatest footwear and carefully arranged hair as their accompaniment. Failing the Muse, this must be my more modest invocation to the "Popolana" of Venice.